#1

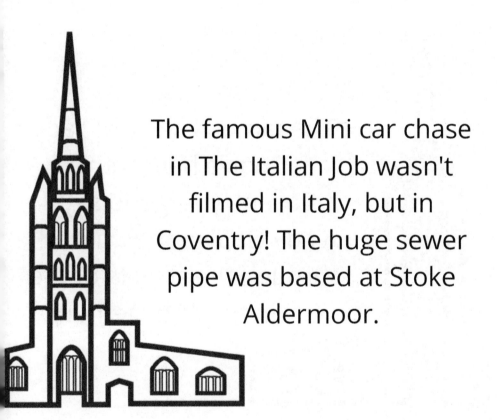

The famous Mini car chase in The Italian Job wasn't filmed in Italy, but in Coventry! The huge sewer pipe was based at Stoke Aldermoor.

#2

The famous story of Lady Godiva hails from Coventry. Legend says Lady Godiva rode naked through the streets of the city in the 11th century.

#3

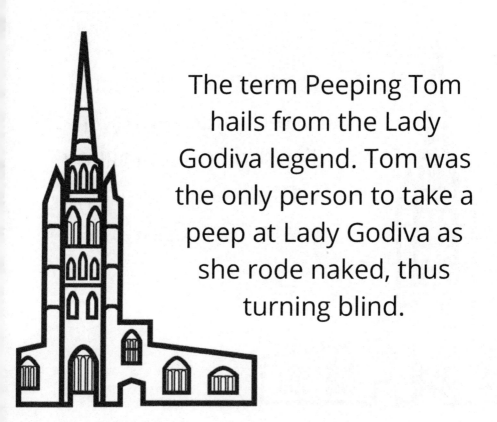

The term Peeping Tom hails from the Lady Godiva legend. Tom was the only person to take a peep at Lady Godiva as she rode naked, thus turning blind.

#4

The UK's car industry started in Coventry, in a disused cotton mill by Gottlieb Daimler in the late 19th Century.

#5

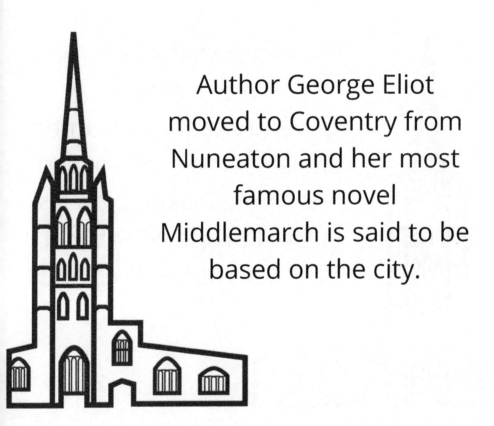

Author George Eliot
moved to Coventry from
Nuneaton and her most
famous novel
Middlemarch is said to be
based on the city.

#6

The bicycle industry is said to have originated in Coventry thanks to James Starley, who modernised the 'boneshaker' bicycles from Europe with metal frames, rubber tires and spokes.

#7

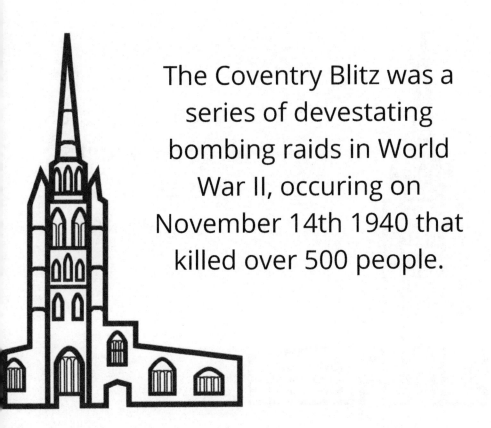

The Coventry Blitz was a series of devestating bombing raids in World War II, occuring on November 14th 1940 that killed over 500 people.

#8

The beloved Christmas film Nativity! and it's sequels is set in and around Coventry

#9

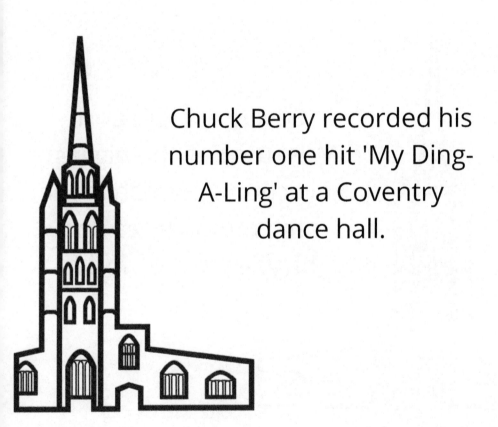

Chuck Berry recorded his number one hit 'My Ding-A-Ling' at a Coventry dance hall.

#10

Coventry Transport Museum has the biggest collection of British made cars, motorcycles and bicycles in the world.

#11

Coventry was the site of the English Parliament on two separate occasions!

#12

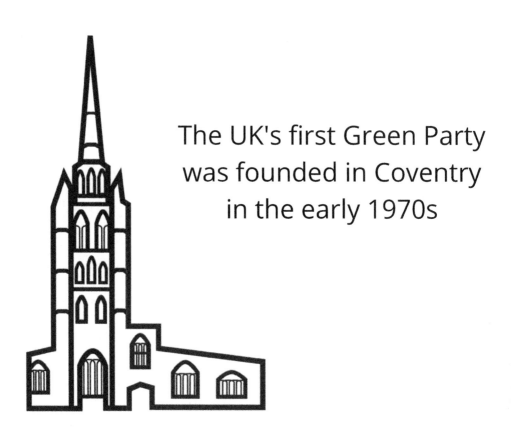

The UK's first Green Party
was founded in Coventry
in the early 1970s

#13

Two-Tone is a huge musical genre and it was created in Coventry. Bands such as The Specials and Selector helped pioneer the movement

#14

After World War II, Coventry led the way in shopping, being the first city in Europe to open a fully traffic-free shopping centre in 1948.

#15

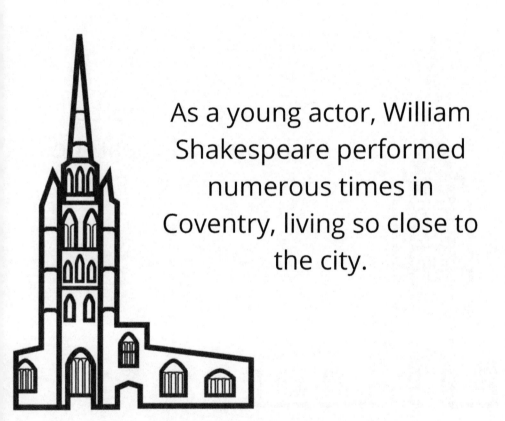

As a young actor, William Shakespeare performed numerous times in Coventry, living so close to the city.

#16

Coventry City Football Club famously beat the odds to raise the FA Cup in 1987

#17

Coventry was awarded the title UK's City of Culture in 2021

#18

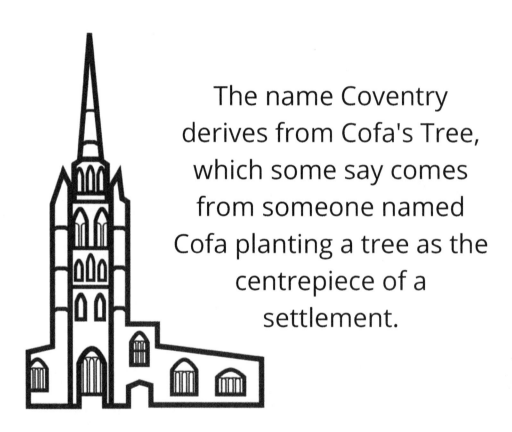

The name Coventry derives from Cofa's Tree, which some say comes from someone named Cofa planting a tree as the centrepiece of a settlement.

#19

Both ribbon and silk weaving were part of the reason Coventry became such a huge industrial city

#20

Alongside the textile industry, Coventry was also a world leader on creating clocks and watches

#21

In 1942 Coventry was removed as county status and redefined as a city

#22

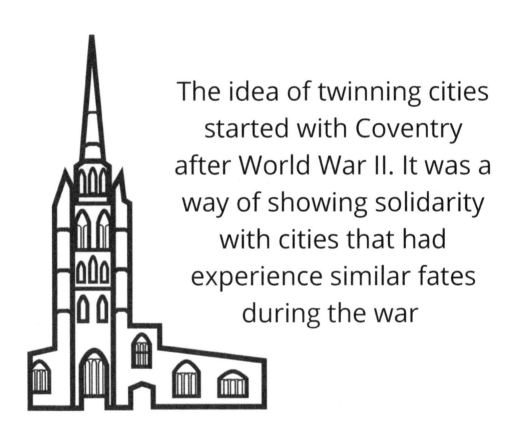

The idea of twinning cities started with Coventry after World War II. It was a way of showing solidarity with cities that had experience similar fates during the war

#23

Stalingrad was the first city to twin with Coventry. This followed with Kiel and Dresden. There are currently 26 cities twinned with Coventry

#24

The current count shows there are over 360,000 people living in Coventry

#25

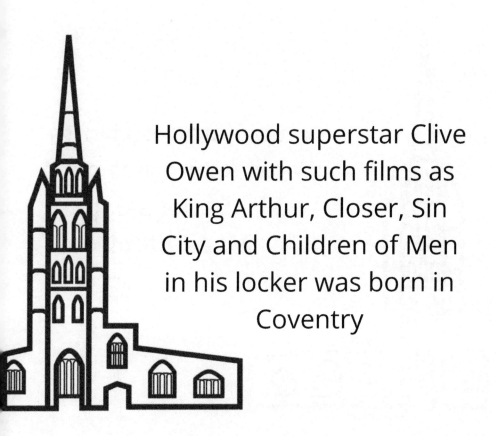

Hollywood superstar Clive Owen with such films as King Arthur, Closer, Sin City and Children of Men in his locker was born in Coventry

#26

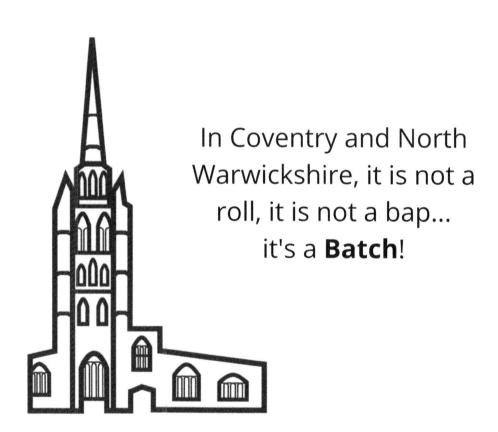

In Coventry and North Warwickshire, it is not a roll, it is not a bap...
it's a **Batch**!

#27

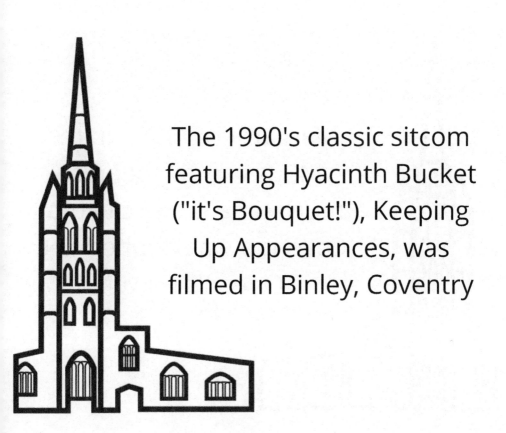

The 1990's classic sitcom featuring Hyacinth Bucket ("it's Bouquet!"), Keeping Up Appearances, was filmed in Binley, Coventry

#28

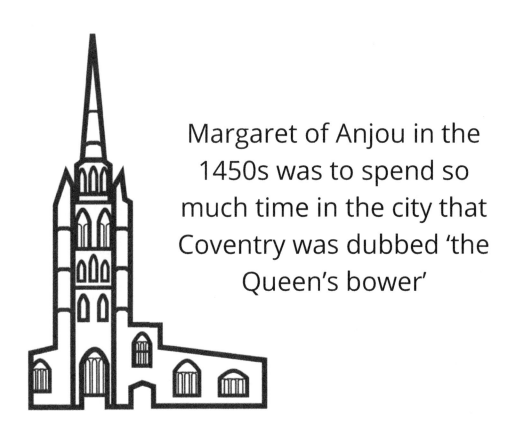

Margaret of Anjou in the
1450s was to spend so
much time in the city that
Coventry was dubbed 'the
Queen's bower'

#29

The UK's very first ethnic minority Policeman Mohammed Daar started his beat on the streets of Coventry in 1966

#30

Coventry is further from the coast than any other city in Britain.

#31

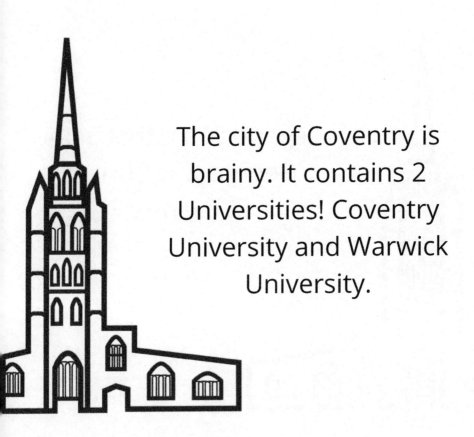

The city of Coventry is brainy. It contains 2 Universities! Coventry University and Warwick University.

#32

Legend has it that Saint George was born in Coventry.

#33

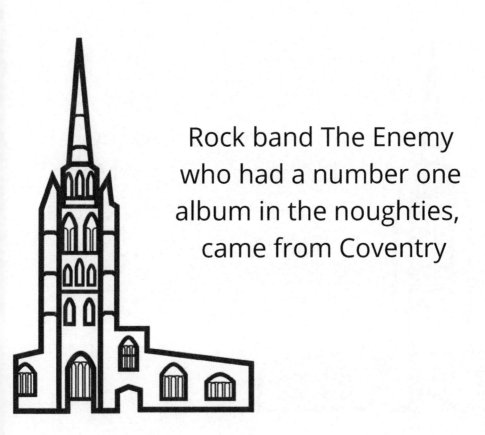

Rock band The Enemy
who had a number one
album in the noughties,
came from Coventry

#34

Coventry was the birthplace of Tom Mann, one of the 'greats' of the trade union movement

#35

After the Coventry Blitz, the city's name entered the German language when Joseph Goebbels used the term coventriert to describe similar levels of destruction of other enemy towns

#36

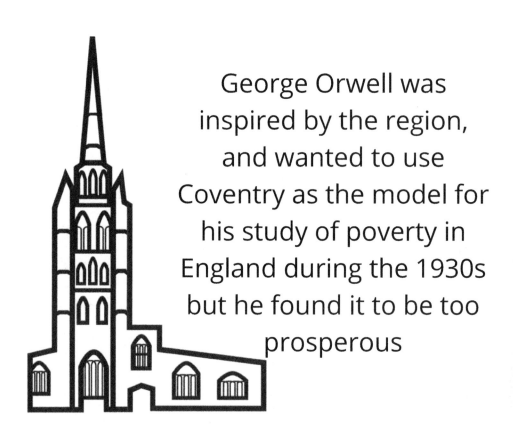

George Orwell was inspired by the region, and wanted to use Coventry as the model for his study of poverty in England during the 1930s but he found it to be too prosperous

#37

Monty Python's first ever live performance was at the Belgrade Theatre in 1971

#38

In October 2005, the late John Lennon's wife Yoko Ono planted two Japanese trees in the Coventry Cathedral gardens

#39

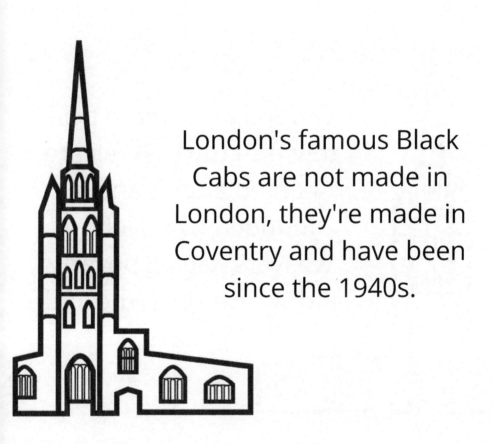

London's famous Black
Cabs are not made in
London, they're made in
Coventry and have been
since the 1940s.

#40

Coventry has three twin towns in the USA. All are named after it and all founded by Coventry weavers fleeing poverty and starvation in the 19th century

#41

Basil Spence's new cathedral, consecrated in 1962 was voted Britain's most popular 20th century building in a national Millennium poll conducted by English Heritage and Channel Four.

#42

The first smokeless zone in Britain was introduced in Coventry in 1948

#43

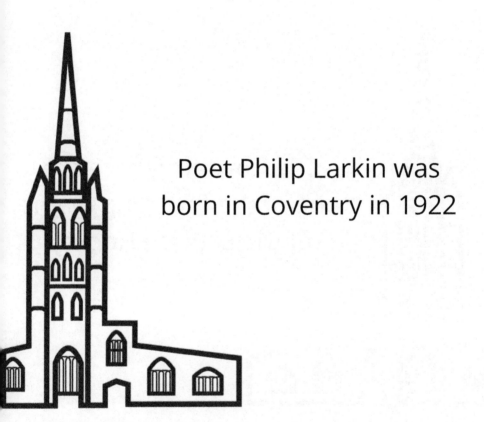

Poet Philip Larkin was born in Coventry in 1922

#44

The Coventry Blaze are one of the founding teams of the Elite Ice Hockey League.

#45

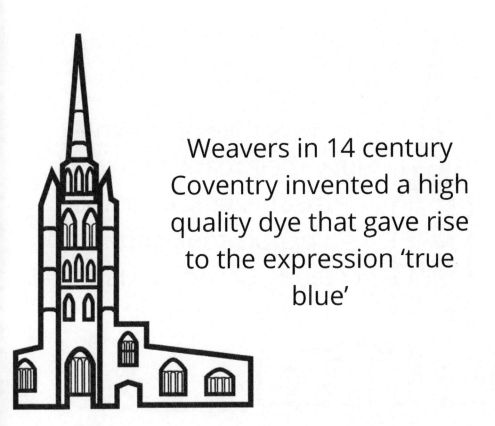

Weavers in 14 century Coventry invented a high quality dye that gave rise to the expression 'true blue'

#46

The people of Coventry love their market so much, that in 2008, over 150 people took part in creating Coventry Market - The Musical!

#47

On several occasions
Coventry was briefly the
capital of England!

#48

The Coventry Carol does in fact originate from Coventry. Who Knew?!

#49

The Belgrade Theatre is the first purpose built civic theatre in the UK

#50

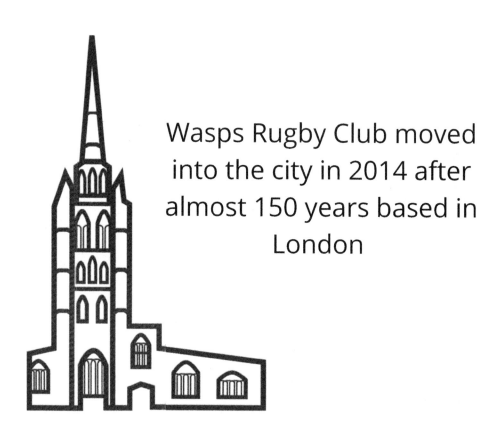

Wasps Rugby Club moved into the city in 2014 after almost 150 years based in London

#51

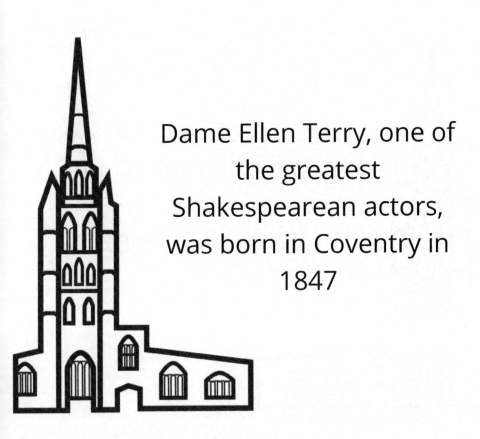

Dame Ellen Terry, one of the greatest Shakespearean actors, was born in Coventry in 1847

#52

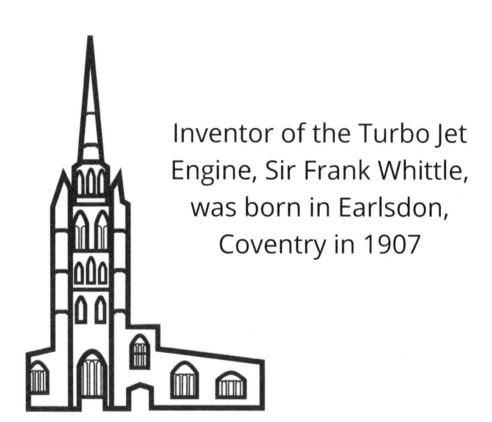

Inventor of the Turbo Jet Engine, Sir Frank Whittle, was born in Earlsdon, Coventry in 1907

#53

Coventry hosts a music festival called Godiva Festival every year with bands such as Supergrass, The Charlatans and The Enemy headlining

#54

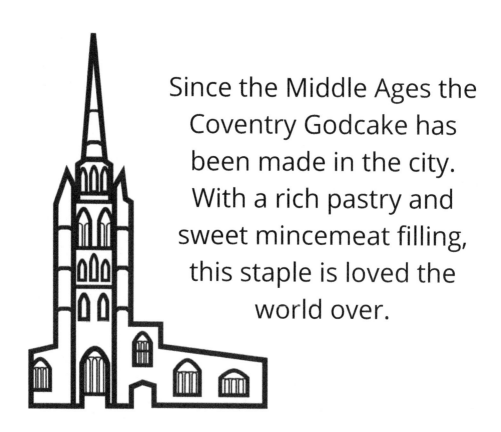

Since the Middle Ages the Coventry Godcake has been made in the city. With a rich pastry and sweet mincemeat filling, this staple is loved the world over.

#55

Coventry's newest water park, The Wave, is home to the UK's largest wave pool.

#56

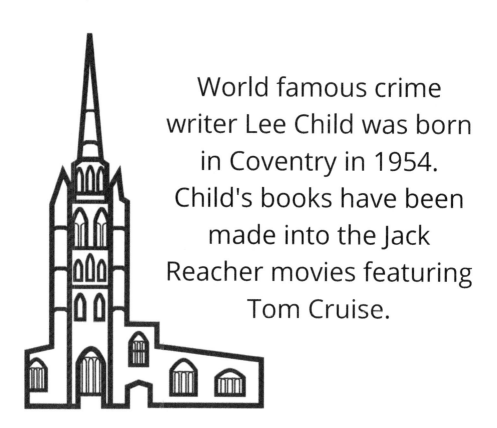

World famous crime writer Lee Child was born in Coventry in 1954. Child's books have been made into the Jack Reacher movies featuring Tom Cruise.

#57

The Doctor Who theme,
known the world over,
was written and recorded
by Coventry musician
Delia Derbyshire.

#58

The Coventry Writers group is one of the UK's longest running writers group, having started in the 1950s.

#59

The spire of St Michael's Church, the old cathedral, at 295 feet is the third tallest in England, after Salisbury and Norwich.

#60

The 500-year-old Coventry Tapestry, on the north wall of the city's medieval guildhall of St Mary, is the oldest in the country still hanging on the wall for which it was made.

#61

Coventry Stadium held BriSCA Formula 1 Stock Cars from 1954 till 2016, the longest serving track in the UK to race continuously.

#62

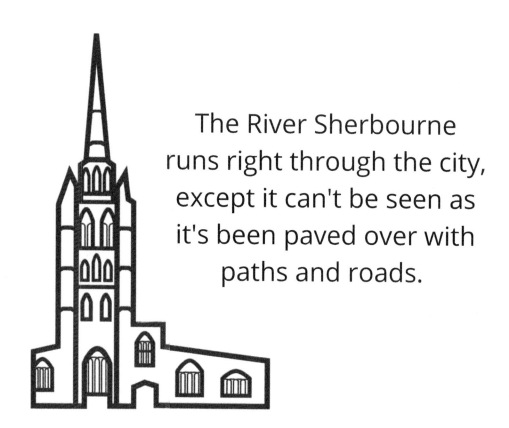

The River Sherbourne runs right through the city, except it can't be seen as it's been paved over with paths and roads.

#63

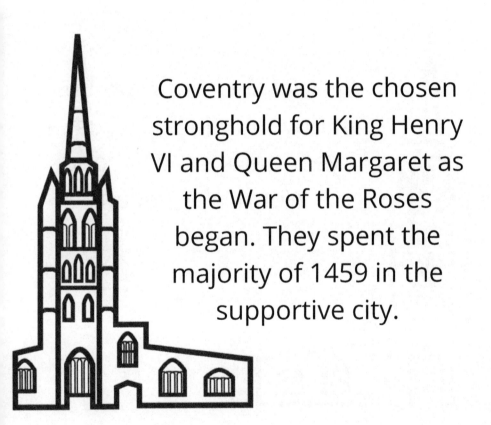

Coventry was the chosen stronghold for King Henry VI and Queen Margaret as the War of the Roses began. They spent the majority of 1459 in the supportive city.

#64

Air-raid shelters were built in Coventry in 1938, just a year before the Second World War began.

#65

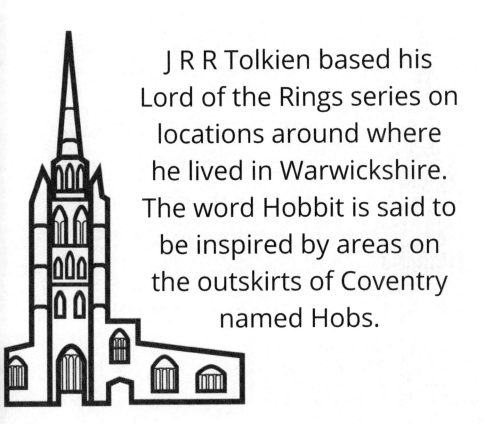

J R R Tolkien based his Lord of the Rings series on locations around where he lived in Warwickshire. The word Hobbit is said to be inspired by areas on the outskirts of Coventry named Hobs.

#66

Mary Queen of Scots was imprisoned in St. Mary's Hall for three months from November 1569 under the orders of Queen Elizabeth I

#67

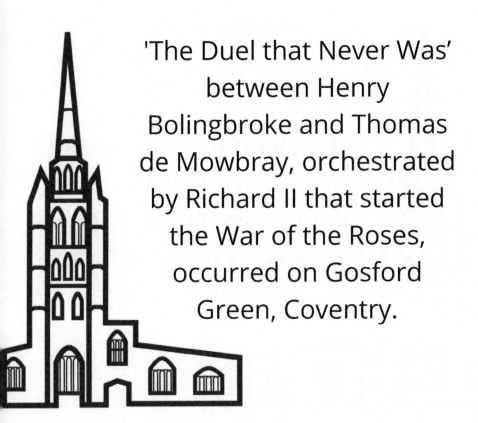

'The Duel that Never Was' between Henry Bolingbroke and Thomas de Mowbray, orchestrated by Richard II that started the War of the Roses, occurred on Gosford Green, Coventry.

#68

The elephant is a Coventry icon that can be seen on lampposts, bollards, drain covers and even in the football club logo.

#69

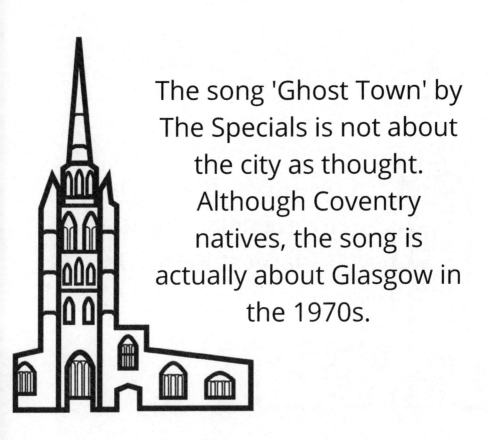

The song 'Ghost Town' by The Specials is not about the city as thought. Although Coventry natives, the song is actually about Glasgow in the 1970s.

#70

Coventry is the 9th largest city in England, and 11th largest in the UK

#71

Coventry is England's Irish Dancing capital, with some people travelling hundreds of miles to learn from the best.

#72

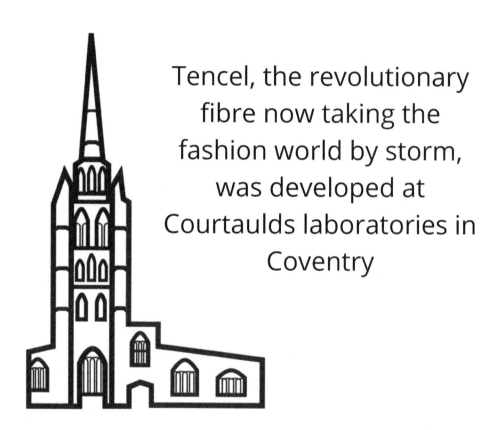

Tencel, the revolutionary fibre now taking the fashion world by storm, was developed at Courtaulds laboratories in Coventry

#73

Dick Whittington was a member of one of Coventry's mediaeval craft guilds

#74

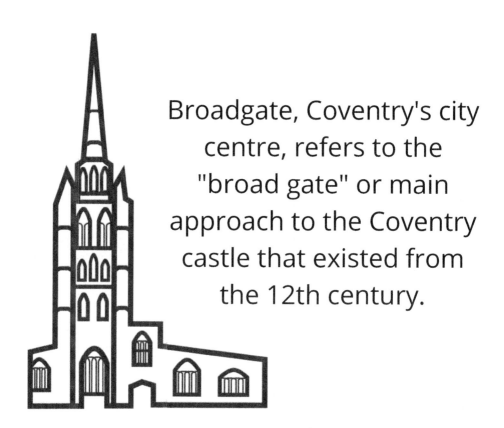

Broadgate, Coventry's city centre, refers to the "broad gate" or main approach to the Coventry castle that existed from the 12th century.

#75

In 1465 the Coventry mint was established where nobles, half-nobles and groats were coined. The building is now The Golden Cross pub.

#76

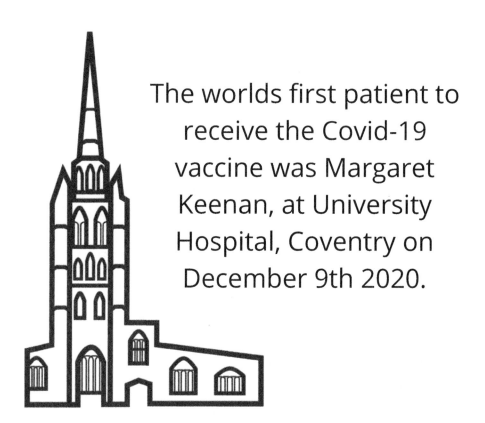

The worlds first patient to receive the Covid-19 vaccine was Margaret Keenan, at University Hospital, Coventry on December 9th 2020.

#77

Over 700 houses were bulldozed to make way for the Coventry Ring Road

#78

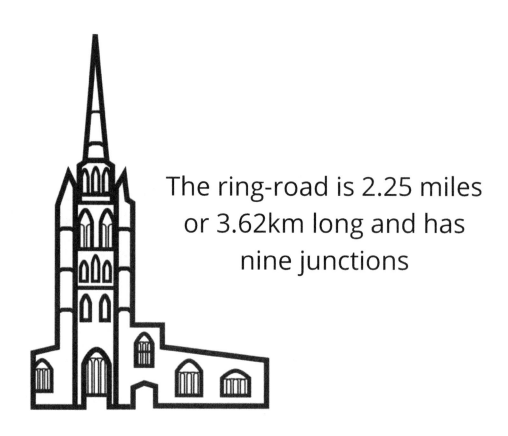

The ring-road is 2.25 miles or 3.62km long and has nine junctions

#79

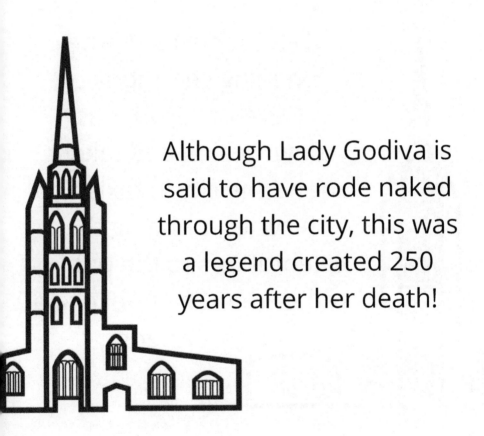

Although Lady Godiva is said to have rode naked through the city, this was a legend created 250 years after her death!

#80

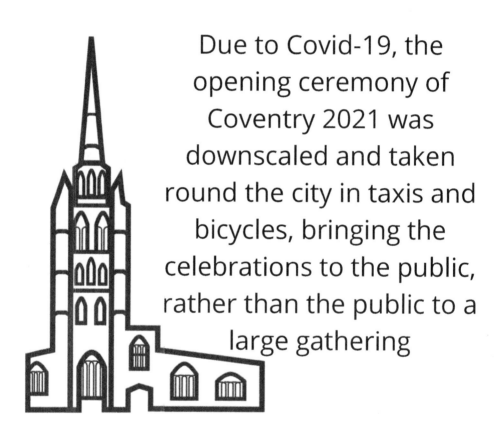

Due to Covid-19, the opening ceremony of Coventry 2021 was downscaled and taken round the city in taxis and bicycles, bringing the celebrations to the public, rather than the public to a large gathering

#81

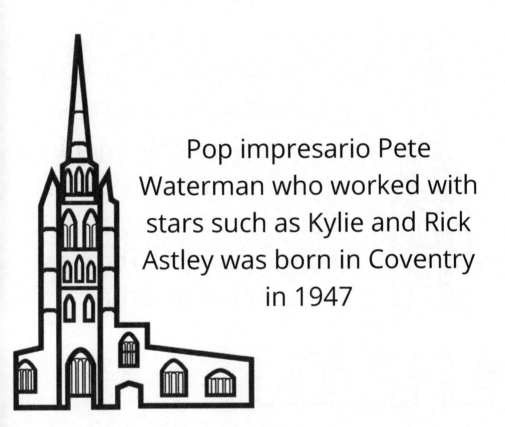

Pop impresario Pete Waterman who worked with stars such as Kylie and Rick Astley was born in Coventry in 1947

#82

Spooks: The Greater Good, the film spin off from the British MI-5 TV series, was filmed in Coventry and featured Game of Thrones star Kit Harington

#83

Coventry City FC have struggled since the turn of the millenium, falling to the lowest proffessional league in England, and at points, playing their home games in Birmingham and Northampton

#84

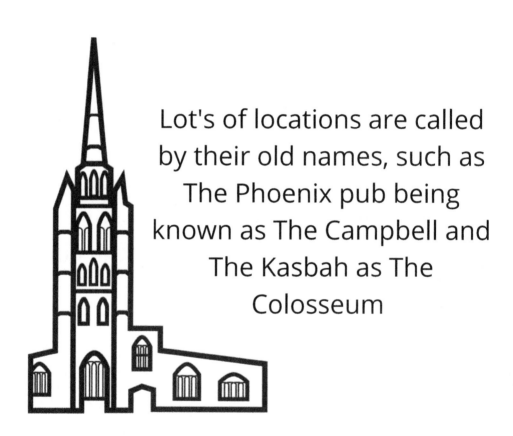

Lot's of locations are called by their old names, such as The Phoenix pub being known as The Campbell and The Kasbah as The Colosseum

#85

Spon Street holds the most important collection of medieval timber-framed buildings in England, as after the Blitz, 10 buildings throughout the city were relocated to Spon Street

#86

In medieval history, Coventry was renowned throughout Europe for its choral music and Bablake Chapel maintained an important choral school.

#87

Novelist Graham Joyce, winner of the O Henry Award is from Keresley. His World Fantasy Award-winning novel "The Facts Of Life" is set in Coventry during the blitz and in the post-war rebuilding period

#88

Coombe Country Park, although outside the city boundary is Coventry City Council's only country park

#89

A video showing a women putting a cat in a wheelie bin went viral in 2010. Yep, this was in Coventry!

#90

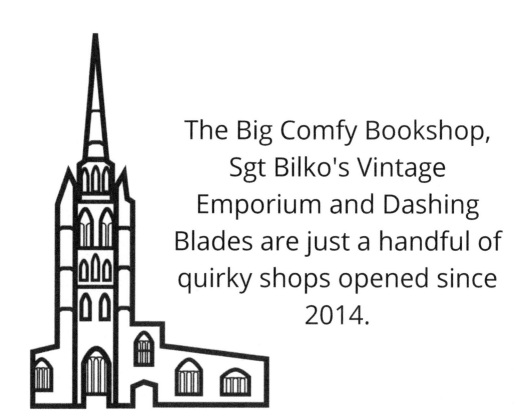

The Big Comfy Bookshop, Sgt Bilko's Vintage Emporium and Dashing Blades are just a handful of quirky shops opened since 2014.

#91

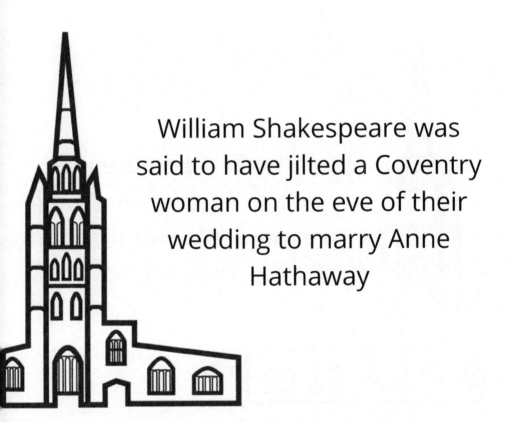

William Shakespeare was said to have jilted a Coventry woman on the eve of their wedding to marry Anne Hathaway

#92

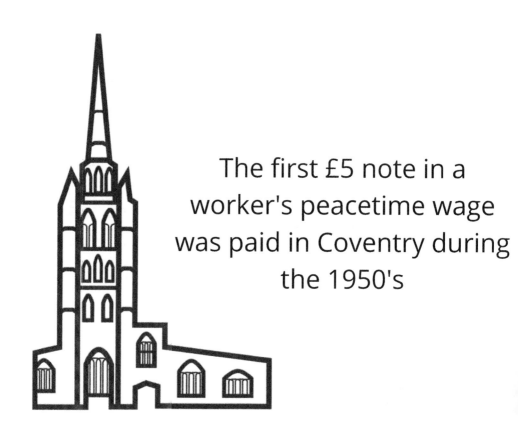

The first £5 note in a worker's peacetime wage was paid in Coventry during the 1950's

#93

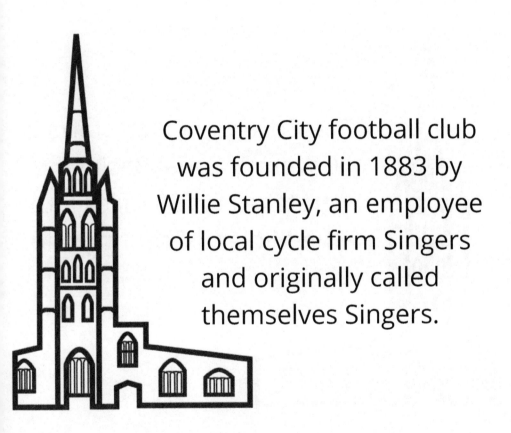

Coventry City football club was founded in 1883 by Willie Stanley, an employee of local cycle firm Singers and originally called themselves Singers.

#94

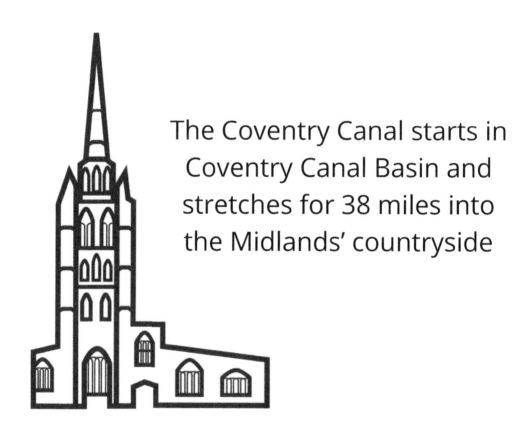

The Coventry Canal starts in Coventry Canal Basin and stretches for 38 miles into the Midlands' countryside

#95

Coventry kid Panjabi MC, rapper and DJ, wrote worldwide bhangra hit "Mundian To Bach Ke", which sold 10 million copies worldwide.

#96

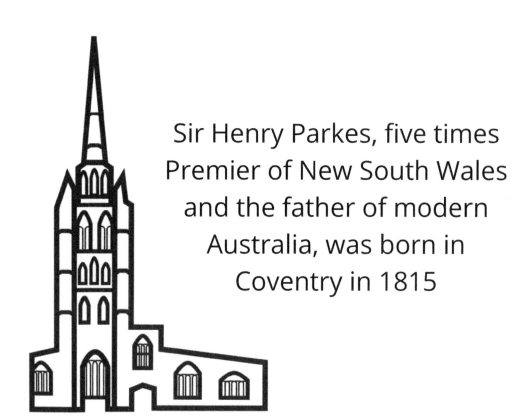

Sir Henry Parkes, five times Premier of New South Wales and the father of modern Australia, was born in Coventry in 1815

#97

Coventry's surviving gatehouse is the oldest building in Britain to be used as a register office.

#98

The city was targeted in WWII due to its high concentration of armaments, munitions and engine plants which contributed greatly to the British war effort

#99

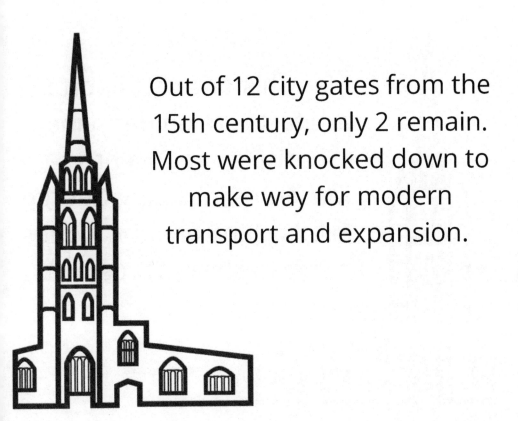

Out of 12 city gates from the 15th century, only 2 remain. Most were knocked down to make way for modern transport and expansion.

#100

Many historically important artefacts are on permanent display at Coventry Museums including George Eliot's piano and the worlds fastest car, Thrust 2

Printed in Great Britain
by Amazon

32707379R00056